# 36 CREATIVE IDEAS For Children in the Church School

# 36 CREATIVE IDEAS For Children in the Church School

**Written and Illustrated by
LOIS BROKERING**

Concordia Publishing House
St. Louis

Scripture quotations marked RSV are from the Revised Standard Version of the Bible, copyrighted 1946, 1952, © 1971, 1973. Used by permission.

The Scripture quotation marked NIV is from The Holy Bible: New International Version, copyright © 1978 by the New York International Bible Society, and published by the Zondervan Corporation, Grand Rapids, MI.

Scripture quotations marked KJV are from the King James Version of the Bible.

Copyright © 1982 Concordia Publishing House
3558 S. Jefferson Avenue, St. Louis, MO 63118
Manufactured in the United States of America
ISBN 0-570-03865-0

2 3 4 5 6 7 8 9 10   CPC   91 90 89 88 87 86 85

For Amy and April and all the children at St. Peter's Lutheran Church, Mesa, Arizona.

# CONTENTS

| | |
|---|---|
| How to Use This Book | 8 |
| 1. Labor Day/Do Lists | 9 |
| 2. Autumnal Equinox/Leaf Motif | 11 |
| 3. Holy Cross Day/Cross Symbol | 13 |
| 4. Halloween and All Saints' Day/Saint Shields | 14 |
| 5. Thanksgiving/Place Mats | 16 |
| 6. Advent/Calendar | 18 |
| 7. Advent/Prayer Tree | 21 |
| 8. Christmas/Sparkly Reflectors | 23 |
| 9. Christmas/Creche | 24 |
| 10. Christmas/Song | 25 |
| 11. Christmas-Epiphany/Story | 28 |
| 12. Candlemas/Candle Holder | 30 |
| 13. Valentine's Day/Heart Decorations | 32 |
| 14. Spring Equinox/Bean Sprouts | 34 |
| 15. Easter/Symbols | 36 |
| 16. Ascension/Balloons and Kites | 38 |
| 17. Pentecost/Church Models | 40 |
| 18. Arbor Day and Mother's and Father's Day/Tree Planting and Parent Party | 42 |

| | | |
|---|---|---|
| **19.** | Trinity/Mobiles | 45 |
| **20.** | Flag Day/Paper Flags | 46 |
| **21.** | Class Banner/Banner Making | 47 |
| **22.** | Mobiles/Personalized Mobiles | 49 |
| **23.** | Pouff Balls/Decorations and Greetings | 51 |
| **24.** | Friendship Album/Classmate Remembrances | 53 |
| **25.** | Bible Story Telling/Six Ways | 55 |
| **26.** | Let's Pretend/Being Somebody Else | 57 |
| **27.** | After School Hours/Things to Do | 59 |
| **28.** | Book Care/Protective Covers | 61 |
| **29.** | School Days/For the Record | 63 |
| **30.** | Last Week of School/Flower Baskets | 65 |
| **31.** | After the School Year Is Over/This Is the Year That Was | 67 |
| **32.** | Summer Solstice/Parades and Picnics | 69 |
| **33.** | Vacation/Third Verse | 71 |
| **34.** | Birds and Butterflies/Origami: American Style | 73 |
| **35.** | Water Paintings/Summer Fun | 75 |
| **36.** | Winter Flowers/Mementos | 77 |

# HOW TO USE THIS BOOK

A school year is a time for growth and changes, nine months of building memories, reaching back into roots and history, but always looking forward to next year . . . "When I'm in fourth grade" . . or "junior high" . . . or "grown up!"

How was it? How will it be? How can we preserve the present to remember when it is our past? How can we make every precious moment of childhood count in ways that develop the creativity that God has placed in each child?

Here are some ideas to help children take a look at how they are spending their time, with suggestions to help them sample many directions for their creativity . . . to help school days be some of the best days of their lives.

All over the world people celebrate festivals, holidays, and the seasons together. The feeling of belonging is one we all need. It will be enlarged when we join with Christian friends and families to celebrate people and events that have rich meaning for our lives together. St. Paul tells us that joy is one of the gifts of the Holy Spirit. Christ encourages us to be of good cheer. Doing things together gives us all a lift from the everyday routine of study and work. It gives us time to attend to our spiritual as well as our physical needs.

We can learn from others as they celebrate life, and we can find what we have in common as the children of God.

This little book gives suggestions for doing many things together—making things, singing, talking about things—as we celebrate life under God and try to grow in our own creativity and better understand ourselves and others.

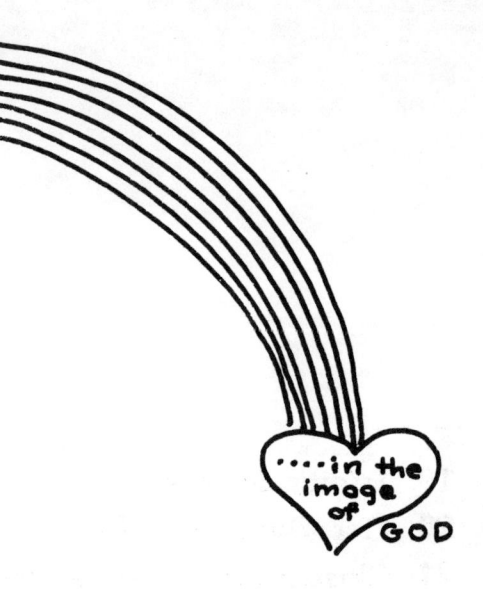

# 1. LABOR DAY

*First Monday in September*

Then He said to His disciples: "The harvest is plentiful, but the laborers are few; pray therefore the Lord of the harvest to send out laborers into His harvest." Matthew 9:37-38 RSV

## A Talk with the Children

This day usually marks the end of summertime activities for most families, and the week when school begins. This is the day when we celebrate for the workers of America. We thank God for all the people who make things, transport them, and sell us all the things we need: food and clothing and heat and light, and for the people who help and protect us.

Think of all the things that must be done to keep your school going, and your home.

## Materials

Pencil and paper.

## Activity

*Make two lists.* One for school, one for your home.

List all the things that must be done to keep it going.

School: teaching, cleaning, heating, preparing food, etc.

Home: cleaning, cooking, laundry, shopping, dishwashing, etc.

After drawing up the lists, talk about them.

Let the children tell what they would like to do to help at school, at home. Decide who is capable of doing what they want to do. Who can help their teachers and parents? Who will do the things no one else wants to? How about taking turns?

We all want to live in a nice house.

We all want to be in a school that runs smoothly.

Part of growing up is becoming more responsible all the time.

## A NEW SONG

HERE IS A NEW SONG FOR YOU TO PLAY AND SING. IT'S FUN TO HAVE SOME MUSIC TO LEARN WITHOUT HAVING TO DO IT FOR YOUR TEACHER!

SCHOOL IS WHERE I SPEND MY DAYS, LEARN-ING SPELL-ING MATH OR PLAYS.

SCHOOL DAYS BRING US FRIENDS YOU SEE: HARD TIMES, GOOD TIMES, MEM-OR-IES!

MAKE UP SOME MORE VERSES

ABOUT
- YOUR FRIENDS
- YOUR SCHOOL
- YOUR TEACHERS
- YOUR FAVORITE ACTIVITIES

CLIMBING ON THE BARS IS FUN
SWINGING IN THE NICE WARM SUN
BEST OF ALL I LIKE THE SLIDE
HERE'S MY BIKE — I'LL TAKE A RIDE.

# 2. AUTUMNAL EQUINOX

*September 22 or 23*

And let us not grow weary in well-doing, for in due season we shall reap, if we do not lose heart. Galatians 6:9 RSV

## A Talk with the Children

If autumn comes can winter be far behind? Today marks the changing of the seasons. We will notice the sun will continue to shine lower in the sky. It will rise later, and set earlier. The leaves of trees and flowers will turn brown, red, and gold. It will become cooler. Fruits and grains and vegetables will be harvested. We can note the changing of the color of the leaves. And we can prepare for cooler days and nights.

## Materials

Leaves, wax paper, warm surfaces.

Leftover fabrics, odds and ends, scissors, needles, and thread.

## Activities

### 1. Leaf motif

Gather collections of colorful fall leaves.

Press them between two sheets of wax paper with a warm iron, or rub with brayer on an electric food warmer.

Use leaf papers for window decorations or for place mats.

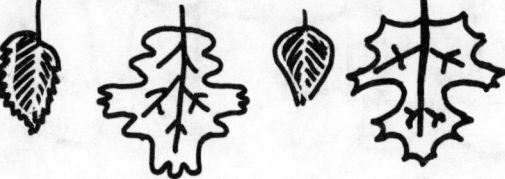

### 2. Snuggle-up

Make one for yourself, or a small one for your little brother or sister. Or your class can make a quilt to give to a poor family, or to a world relief organization.

Collect pieces of fabrics, and nylon stockings and panty hose. Cut nine-inch squares of fabric, sew two pieces together, on all four sides, leaving a three-inch opening on one side.

Stuff a pair of nylons into the pocket, make tiny stitches to close up the opening. Make many more of these out of different pieces of materials. Six, nine, a dozen or more. Sew little designs over each of the squared pockets with large stitches. Sew your pocket squares together with tiny stitches. When you have enough (it depends on how big you want your crazy snuggle-up to be) form them into a blanket or a sack. Now someone will have a warm place while they read a book on a cold winter's evening.

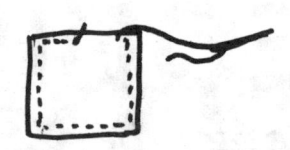

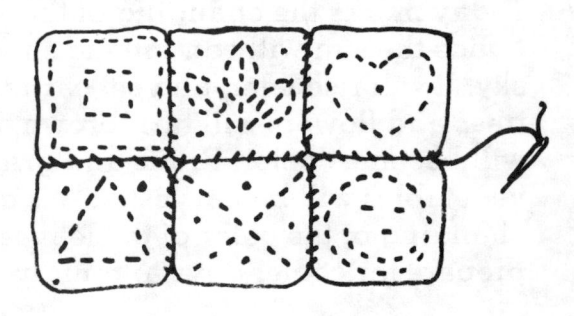

# 3. HOLY CROSS DAY
*September 14*

Then Jesus said to His disciples: "If anyone would come after me, he must deny himself and take up his cross and follow me." Matthew 16:24 NIV

## A Talk with the Children

Look around you. Everywhere you can see crosses. In your rooms, on top of churches, on altars. Why do we wear crosses? put them on walls? A cross is a symbol that shows we love Jesus. It is not magic. It reminds us that Christ is our Savior.

## Materials

Pictures from magazines, posterboard or cardboard from cartons. Glue or paste, or rubber cement. Scissors.

## Activity

*Make a new cross to hang in your room or in your home.*

Look in old magazines for pictures for a collage.

Cut out the pictures. You can cut out words, too.

Place these together to form a cross on a posterboard or cardboard. Glue these down. Cut the board in the shape of a cross. There are many shapes or patterns that represent the cross of Christ.

Tape a pop can ring or a paper clip at the top so you can hang it up.

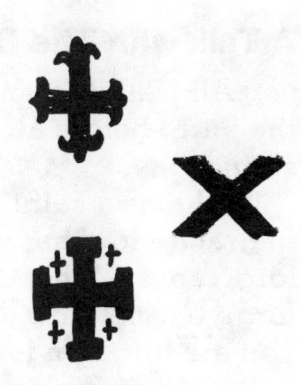

13

# 4. HALLOWEEN ALL SAINTS' DAY

*October 31 and November 1*

For I have derived much joy and comfort from your love, my brother, because the heart of the saints have been refreshed through you. Philemon 7 RSV

## A Talk with The Children

All Hallow E'en abbreviated is Hallowe'en. It is the night before all hallowed ones' (holy ones' or saints) day.

What is a saint? Someone who lives or has lived in grace—in other words, who lived in Christ's forgiveness. What does it mean to live in forgiveness? How do you behave when you know you are forgiven for wrongdoing? Do you really believe your sins are forgiven?

## Materials

Poster paper, construction paper, posterboard. Scissors and glue.

## Activity

*Shield posters of saints*

Let each child choose a saint to honor. Each should sketch a design and choose materials to assemble.

Designs indicated for Andrew, James, Mark, Jude, John, John the Baptist, Paul, and Luke.

ASSEMBLE all the MATERIALS YOU'LL NEED and LET EACH GUEST CHOOSE A DIFFERENT SAINT TO WORK ON.

ST. ANDREW the FIRST CHRISTIAN MISSIONARY.

brother of John ST. JAMES one of the diciples

ST. MARK

A boat is the symbol for ST. JUDE who Sailed around to many places to tell the GOOD NEWS.

ST. JOHN

JOHN and JAMES were sometimes called the "SONS of THUNDER"

ST. JoHN THE BAPTIST

THIS IS A DIFFERENT JOHN. How many boys do you know with the name JOHN?

ST. PAUL

ST. LUKE was a doctor. He probably wrote the books of LUKE and Acts in the BIBLE.

LOOK IN YOUR CHURCH LIBRARY FOR BOOKS ON SAINTS.

What symbol would you choose for yourself as a SAINT?

# 5. THANKSGIVING

*Fourth Thursday of November*

Let us come into His presence with thanksgiving; let us make a joyful noise to Him with songs of praise! Psalm 95:2 RSV

**A Talk with the Children**

Most celebrations and holidays are either national or religious. Thanksgiving is both. Many other cultures and countries have a festival to celebrate the harvest—thanking God for his loving care for another year, for one more harvest, for the gift of food.

The Jewish holiday is called Sukkot. Jesus probably celebrated this feast in September or October.

The Moslems' thanksgiving festival is called Ashura. Celebrants recall that the human race was saved when Noah and his family lived through the flood.

Kwanza is an African thanksgiving and is celebrated by some Black Americans today. It stresses family unity and means "firstfruits." In Old Testament times, firstfruits were given by the Hebrews to God. This is where the practice of tithing began.

## Materials

Construction paper, felt pens, scissors, paste, old magazines.

## Activity

1. Place mats

Let the children look in magazines for pictures of things for which they should be especially grateful for the year past. Give each of them a 12" x 18" sheet of heavy paper. Have them cut out and paste the pictures in a pattern. They may draw additional pictures. Write a prayer, printing it carefully between the pictures. May be used as place mats.

2. Prayer

Thank You for food. Thank You for love.
Thank You for sending Your Son from above.
Thank You for all the beauty I see.
Thank You especially for making me.

# 6. ADVENT

*Four weeks before Christmas*

Readings for each day in Advent

## A Talk with the Children

We are going to read some verses from the Bible each day in Advent that give a promise of God that He would send a Savior, His Son Jesus.

## Materials

Bible, posterboard, ink or colored pencils.
Advent wreath may be lit during readings, if available.

## Activity

Draw four rows of seven squares or circles on posterboard.

Write in one of the Scripture selections in each square.

The *Advent calendar* may be as elaborate as you choose to make it, with symbols of Advent and Christmas.

An Advent wreath may be used during the readings, lighting the candles when the child is reading the selection.

1. LIGHT THE FIRST CANDLE ON YOUR ADVENT WREATH. LEARN THE FIRST VERSE OF A CHRISTMAS CAROL.

2. READ: GENESIS 2:8,9; and GENESIS 3.

3. READ: GENESIS FROM 6:5 TO THE END OF 8.

4. READ: GENESIS 9:8-17

5. READ: GENESIS 22:1-14

6. READ: GENESIS 22:15 to end of chapter.

7. READ: GENESIS 28: 10-22.

8. LIGHT TWO CANDLES. LEARN THE SECOND VERSE OF THE CAROL YOU CHOSE LAST SUNDAY

9. READ: GENESIS 44.

10. READ: EXODUS 1:6 to EXODUS 3:12.

11. READ: EXODUS 20

12. READ: ISAIAH 9:2; LUKE 1:76-79

13. READ: ISAIAH 11:1-9

14. ISAIAH 54:7-9; EXODUS 12:5; MARK 14:12; JOHN 1:29; I CORINTHIANS 5:7(b); REVELATION 21:22-27.

15. LIGHT THREE CANDLES. CHOOSE ANOTHER CAROL YOU'D LIKE TO LEARN AND MEMORIZE THE FIRST VERSE.

16. READ: LUKE 1: 5-25

17. READ: LUKE 1: 26-38

18. READ: LUKE 1: 39-56

19. READ: MATTHEW 1: 18-25

20. READ: LUKE 2: 1-7

21. READ: LUKE 2: 8-14

22. LIGHT FOUR CANDLES. CHRISTMAS IS NEARLY HERE! MEMORIZE ANOTHER VERSE OF THE SECOND CAROL.

23. READ: LUKE 2: 8-20

24. READ: JOHN 10: 11-15

25. READ: MATTHEW 2: 1,2; 7-10.

26. READ: MATTHEW 2: 1-6.

27. READ: MATTHEW 2: 7-12.

28. READ: MATTHEW 2: 13-23.

♡ YOU MAY WANT TO DRAW A PICTURE EACH DAY OF ONE THING THE BIBLE READING TOLD ABOUT — SUCH AS THE MANGER ON DAY 20, A FIVE POINTED STAR ON DAY 25, BABY MOSES IN A BASKET ON DAY 10, etc. ♡

# 7. ADVENT

*Four weeks before Christmas*

Prepare the way of the Lord, make His paths straight. Matthew 3:3 RSV

## A Talk with the Children

Advent is the first festival season of the church year. It is a time to get ready for the coming of Christ at Christmas. It begins the fourth Sunday before Christmas. We should prepare our hearts to receive God's great gift, His Son, Jesus, our Savior.

## Materials

Christmas wrapping paper and cards, construction papers, Scotch tape, glue, and posterboard. Scissors.

## Activity

*Advent prayer tree*

Make a prayer tree for the days of Advent, either for your own room or home or for your schoolroom.

Cut out 28 paper circles from colored paper. Write the names of people: family, friends, church workers, school workers for whom you think prayers should be offered.

Cut out 28 more circles from gift wrap or Christmas card pictures. Make loops of cellophane tape to stick the first set of circles to the second, covering the names.

Arrange the double set of circles into a tree, starting with one at the top row, two in the second, three in the next, etc., ending with two for the trunk. Glue the circles arranged as a tree onto a piece of posterboard. Decorate the edges.

Each day, remove one of the top 28 circles. Pray a special prayer for the person whose name is revealed.

21

**HANUKKAH** is an ancient festival from old testament times which celebrates religious freedom.

— celebrate by eating traditional potato pancakes During the meal talk about what your family would do if someone tried to <u>make</u> you go to a different church — or none at all, or <u>make</u> you worship a different God.

LIGHT 8 CANDLES

— THINK of things that keep people away from their God today:
- sport, trips, recreation
- television
- earning money
- what else can you think of?

HOW CAN WE FIGHT THESE LIKE THE JEWS FOUGHT BACK WHEN ANTIOCHUS, THE SYRIAN KING, DROVE THEM OUT OF THE TEMPLE IN JERUSALEM?

Hanukkah means dedication — CAN YOU DEDICATE YOUR LIFE TO GOD?

# 8. CHRISTMAS

I am the Light of the world; he who follows Me will not walk in darkness, but will have the light of life. John 8:12 RSV

## A Talk with the Children

Look for Christmas lights. How many different kinds can you find? Christmas is often called the festival of lights. What shall we do to get ready for this BIG celebration?

## Materials

Paper, cellophane tapes, needle and thread, glue, aluminum wrap, glitter, Epsom salts.

## Activity

*Sparkly reflectors*

Make some sparkly reflectors to remind you to reflect Christ's light.

Cut heavy paper (like colored construction paper) into interesting shapes. Cut circles, diamonds, stars, or tree forms. Thread a needle and make loops for hanging from light fixtures, furniture, mirrors, etc. Paint the shapes with white glue and sprinkle with Epsom salts and glitter.

Punch holes in some double shapes, insert colored cellophane between them and glue together.

Hang your "light" ornaments everywhere.

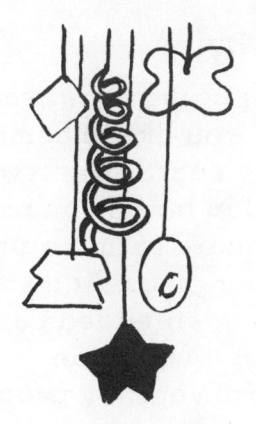

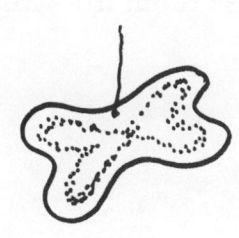

# 9. CHRISTMAS

The people who sat in darkness have seen a great light. Matthew 4:16 RSV

## A Talk with the Children

What is a Christmas creche?
It is a little scene of Jesus' birth in a stable.
What were stables like in Bible times?
Have you ever been on a farm with a barn? Describe it.
Let's read the story of the shepherds and the angels. Luke 2.

## Materials

Thin boards or plywood, or heavy cardboard.
Straw, grass, or shredded plastic or paper.
Toy people, or makeup cardboard figures.

## Activity

*Building a Christmas creche*
If you like to hammer and saw, make a creche of thin boards or plywood. Use a grocery carton sliced in half if you prefer. Fold a heavy piece of cardboard to make a roof, and extend the floor with another piece. Add some straw, or substitute dead grass or shredded paper or Easter basket grass. Fasten it with glue.

Use your toy people for Mary and Joseph and the shepherds.

Add some toy animals. If you don't have any, make them out of cardboard, draw them and color, or dress them up with pieces of material.

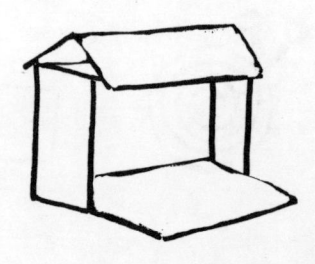

# 10. CHRISTMAS

Arise, shine; for your light has come, and the glory of the Lord has risen upon you. Isaiah 60:1 RSV

## A Talk with the Children

Here is a new song for us to learn.

We can sing it when we read Luke 2, between verses 7 and 8.

## Materials

This song could be sung after the creche has been constructed.

This song might be incorporated if the group is going to "act out" the Christmas story. It may be sung by Mary or the angels.

The "birthday" song will be more effective if sung by two groups.

# A SONG TO USHER CHRISTMAS IN

HOW ☆ WHERE ☆ WHO ☆ WHAT ☆ WHEN? DECEMBER 25!

Some-thing's com-ing! (Some-thing's com-ing!) What can it be? (What can it be?)

Je-sus' birth-day, Je-sus' birth-day For you and for me! (For you and for me!)

TWO GROUPS — OR TWO CHILDREN — CAN SING THE SONG. THE SECOND VOICE CAN DO THE REPETITION — THE WORDS IN PARENTHESES.

Make up some actions — movement — dance — fingers!

Learn one verse each week in Advent.

Advent means coming —
- a special event is coming
- a birthday celebration
- the most important birthday ever

♡ HERE IS A NEW SONG FOR YOU TO LEARN ♡

CAN YOU SING IT WHEN

- You're reading Luke 2 — between verses 7 and 8?
- You're feeling too excited about Christmas coming and you want to calm down?
- You're acting out the Christmas story? Will the angels sing it? Mary?
- You're enjoying your creche — perhaps in candlelight.

SING IT SOFTLY AND SLOWLY — THE BABY IS ASLEEP!

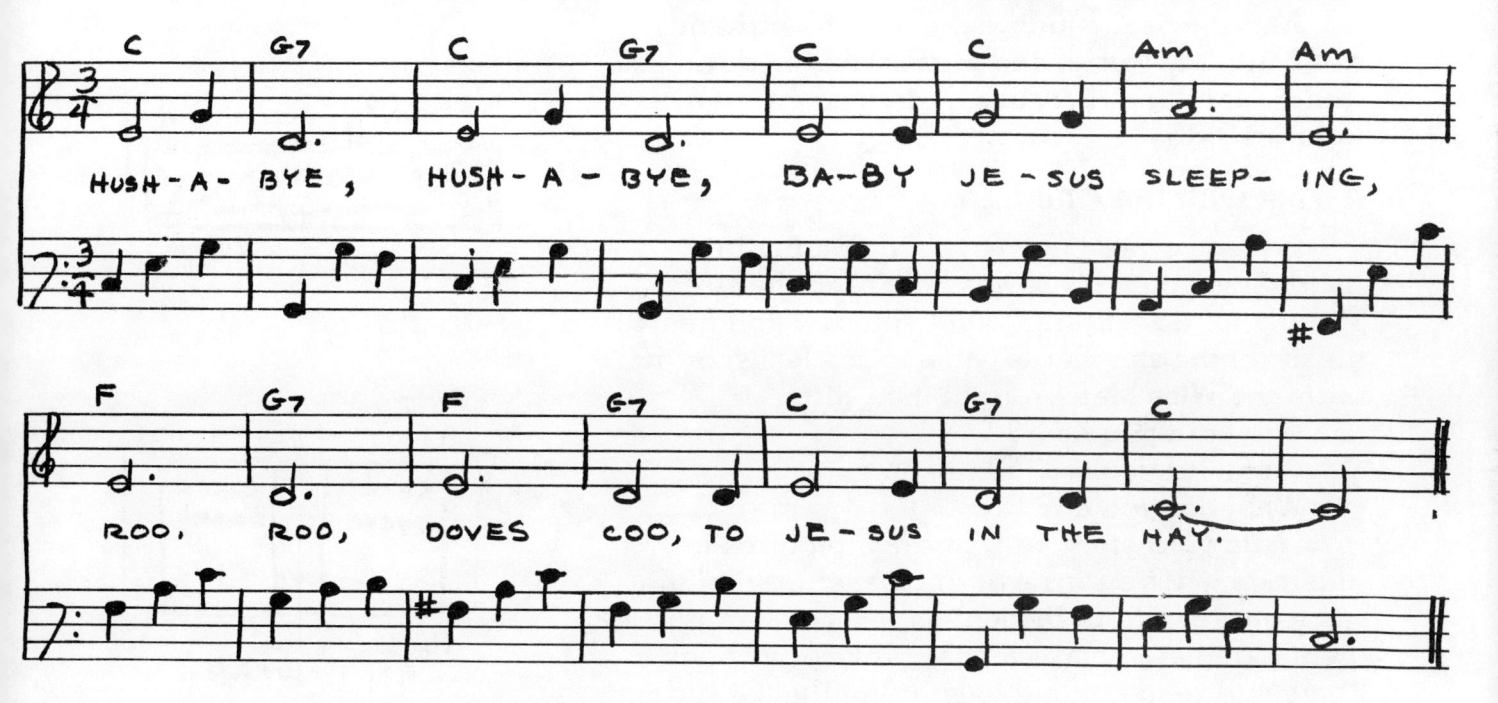

HUSH-A-BYE, HUSH-A-BYE, BA-BY JE-SUS SLEEP-ING,

ROO, ROO, DOVES COO, TO JE-SUS IN THE HAY.

IF YOU'RE TAKING PIANO LESSONS —
 CAN YOU LEARN TO PLAY IT IN TIME FOR YOUR FAMILY CHRISTMAS CELEBRATION? OR:
 TO ACCOMPANY YOUR SUNDAY SCHOOL CLASS? OR:
 JUST FOR SOMETHING FUN TO DO WHILE SCHOOL IS OUT?
 IF IT'S <u>TOO HARD</u> TO PLAY — JUST DO THE TOP LINE.

IF YOU'RE LEARNING TO PLAY THE GUITAR OR AUTOHARP, TRY THE CHORDS.

How does it sound played on bottles?

CAN YOU MAKE UP SOME MORE VERSES?
 WHAT ANIMALS MIGHT HAVE BEEN THERE BESIDES THE DOVES? WHAT MIGHT THEY HAVE SAID OR DONE?

# 11. CHRISTMAS EPIPHANY

And this is the judgment, that the light has come into the world, and men loved the darkness rather than light, because their deeds were evil. John 3:19:RSV

**A Talk with the Children**

Pretend your dad was the innkeeper in Bethlehem when Jesus was born. Tell the story about your adventures (what you saw and heard) the night the shepherds came to see Jesus, or the night the Wise Men brought their gifts.

What did you hear?
What did you see?
What did you do?

Write your story and/or draw pictures to illustrate it. If you write or draw each part of the story on a separate sheet of paper, you can put them together to make a book. Take your book home and read it aloud to your family. (Grandma would *love* a gift like that from you.)

**Materials**

Paper, wrapping paper (Christmas), cardboard, yarn, paste.

**Activity**

*Writing the Christmas story. Bind the pages into a book.*

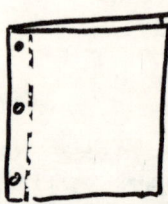

♡ YOU CAN BIND YOUR BOOK THIS WAY:

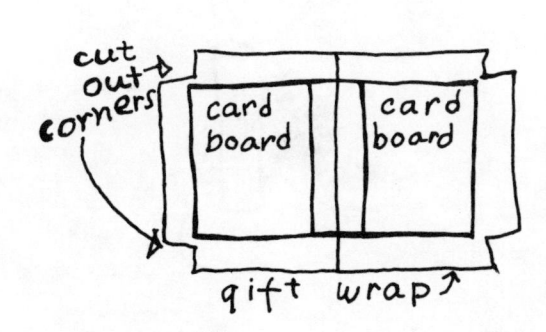

— CUT TWO PIECES OF CARDBOARD THE SAME SIZE AS YOUR PAPER. THEN CUT OFF A ONE INCH WIDE STRIP ALONG ONE SIDE OF EACH PIECE.
— CUT A PIECE OF CHRISTMAS GIFT WRAP PAPER AN INCH BIGGER ALL AROUND THAN THE TWO PIECES OF CARDBOARD TOGETHER, INCLUDING THE STRIPS.

— LAY THE CARDBOARD ON TOP OF THE INSIDE OF THE GIFT WRAP, WITH THE TWO STRIPS AT THE CENTER. Put paste on the edges of the gift wrap that are sticking out, and fold it carefully over the cardboard.
— WHEN THE PASTE IS DRY, FOLD THE COVER IN HALF. PUT THREE HOLES ALONG THE STRIPS, WHICH ARE NOW ON THE EDGE. (You can use notebook paper for a guide.) PUNCH HOLES IN YOUR STORY PAGES TOO. Put them inside the cover.

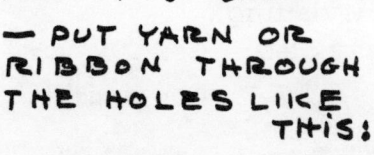

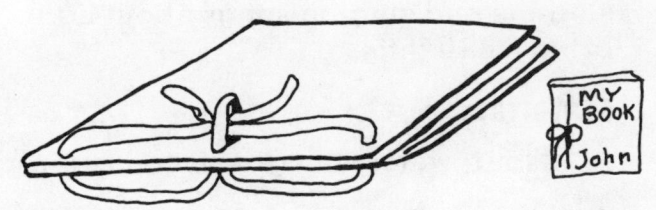

— PUT YARN OR RIBBON THROUGH THE HOLES LIKE THIS:

START BY FOLDING THE YARN IN HALF AND POKING THE FOLD THROUGH THE CENTER HOLE. PUT EACH END THROUGH AN END HOLE, AND THEN THROUGH THAT CENTER LOOP FROM OPPOSITE DIRECTIONS. PULL UP TIGHT AND TIE A BOW

# 12. CANDLEMAS

*Early February*

A light to lighten the Gentiles, and the glory of Thy people Israel. Luke 2:32 KJV

## A Talk with the Children

Candlemas celebrates the ancient Jewish custom of taking children to the temple 40 days after their birth. Read about Christ's first visit to the temple when you light your candles: Luke 2:22-35. In some churches all the candles that will be used throughout the church that year will be blessed. In Luxembourg children celebrate this day by visiting shut-ins and singing songs about light. They also bring small gifts.

## Materials

Flour, water with green food coloring, salt.

## Activity

Mix thoroughly one cup of flour, half cup of salt, half cup of water with green food coloring.

Mix and knead five or ten minutes until smooth and pliable. Add more flour if sticky, water if crumbly.

Shape into a ball and insert a candle.

Stick in bits of natural items if you have some: shells, small cones, pods, and seeds, or bits of green from shrubs and trees, and a tiny ribbon bow. Be sure these items are on the candleholder and not the candle.

**Song**

*Little candles burning bright, what do I think when I see your light? I think of Christ, God's gift to me, who came to earth to make me free.*

A little song to sing while watching the candles burn.

Make up some more verses.

**Christ Candle**

Another way to celebrate Candlemas is on the anniversary of your baptism. If you did not receive one at your baptism, get a special candle and light it each year on this special birthday in Christ.

**At Home**

MAKE A CANDLE (by recycling)

Gather up all the old candle stubs you can find. Put them in a clean can from tomato sauce or mushrooms. Melt them by placing the can in hot (NEVER boiling) water. Use low heat — or an electric appliance, and do this ONLY with an adult nearby to help. Continue adding old stubs until the can is full. Bury or remove the old wicks — except one — which you can pull up in the center. Cool. Decorate the can.

GROUND-HOGS DAY — February 2  Unless you live in the southern part of our country — your chances of seeing a ground hog who isn't hibernating are SLIM. Rest assured that winter will still hang around awhile whether it's sunny or not. Celebrate by getting a new winter hat or long-sleeve shirt at an end-of-winter sale, or wash all your mittens!

# 13.
# VALENTINE'S DAY
*February 14*

A friend loveth at all times, and a brother is born for adversity. Proverbs 17:17 KJV

## A Talk with the Children

St. Valentine's Day is February 14, which is the day St. Valentine was put to death because he was a Christian. St. Valentine was a good friend to a little blind girl whose father was his jailer. Legend tells us he is supposed to have restored her sight, and sent her a farewell note signed: "From Your Valentine."

## Materials

Various colored poster and construction papers. Scissors, transparent tape.

## Activities

*Make various constructions, mobiles, and decorations for the classroom, and for one's own room at home.*

CUT TWO HEART SHAPES FROM HEAVY PAPER SUCH AS CONSTRUCTION PAPER. SLIT ONE HALFWAY FROM THE TOP, THE OTHER HALF WAY FROM THE BOTTOM on the center fold. SLIP ONE HEART over the other so the centers are together, the two slits overlapping — Tape the hearts so they stay perpendicular to each other.

Cut out lots of hearts in several kinds of paper.

Fasten your hearts together in as many ways as you can think of.

USE PAPER LACE TOO.

Tape ribbons to the sides and point so they hang down. Paste lots of hearts in many sizes onto the ribbons.

HANG YOUR HEARTS FOR A DECORATION, OR GIVE THEM AS A GIFT.

Making your own valentines is lots of fun. Giving them to friends is even more fun.

FASTEN SOME WITH PAPER SPRINGS!

- cut some strips 1/2" x 8"
- paste into an L shape
- FOLD the GREEN ONE DOWN over the white one
- FOLD THE WHITE ONE across the green one.
- FOLD THE GREEN one up over the white one.
- FOLD THE white one over the green one. Continue till all the paper is used. FASTEN with a dot of glue or paste.

USE TWO COLORS TILL YOU CAN DO IT EASILY

USE LONGER STRIPS to make ARMS & LEGS.

ST. PATRICK was not Irish! He was a MISSIONARY who went to IRELAND and SPENT THIRTY YEARS TELLING PEOPLE ABOUT JESUS — way back in the year 432.

MARCH 17

St. Pat used the shamrock to help people understand GOD. Now it is a SYMBOL of IRELAND, and of St. Patrick too.

# 14. SPRING

And He said: So is the kingdom of God, as if a man should cast seed into the ground, and should sleep, and rise night and day, and the seed should spring and grow up, he knoweth now how. Mark 4:26-27 KJV

## A Talk with the Children

Spring begins officially—if not always actually—on March 21. Celebrate the spring equinox with a walk through your neighborhood, looking for the first signs of green things growing. The vernal equinox is one of the two times each year when the sun crosses the heavenly equator. This is the day in March when the length of the day and the night are approximately the same number of hours.

## Materials

Mung beans or alfalfa seeds.
Paper towels, baking dish, plastic wrap.

## Activity

*Growing plants:* an activity for home or the classroom.

Buy some seeds and grow them in a dish in four or five days.

They can be incorporated in a salad.

## Prayer Poem

THANKS FOR MAKING GREEN, DEAR GOD,
THE LOVELY COLOR OF THE SOD,
THE TREES AND PLANTS I EAT AND SEE:
THE BEST OF COLORS PLANNED FOR ME.

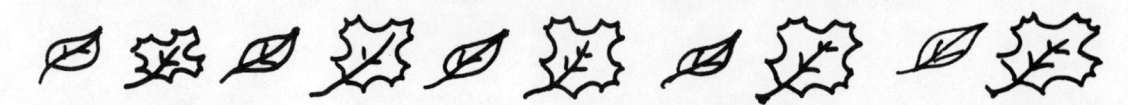

## MARCH 21

CELEBRATE
 the SPRING EQUINOX
  with a big green salad!
   SPROUT SOME SEEDS — mung beans or alfalfa are good.

BUY the seeds at a co-op or health food store if your grocery does not carry them.

♣ Soak a teaspoon of seeds in water overnight. Pour off the water in the morning.

♣ Put a folded paper towel in the bottom of a baking dish. Dampen — but don't SOAK it.

♣ SPRINKLE THE SEEDS EVENLY over the damp towel. Cover the dish with a piece of plastic wrap. 6×10"

♣ Once a day lift the plastic to let in some fresh air, then fasten it against the dish again. In 4 or 5 days you should have fresh green sprouts to mix with your salad.

# 15. EASTER

Ye seek Jesus of Nazareth, which was crucified; He is risen, He is not here. Behold the place where they laid Him. Mark 16:6

## A Talk with the Children

Easter is never on the same date each year.
Easter falls on the first Sunday following the full moon after March 21.
There are many symbols for Easter that we use in our customs, greetings, and gifts. Three that are most popular are: the Easter lily that blooms in the spring—a common and popular symbol of our Lord's resurrection; the Easer egg—a symbol of Jesus Christ coming forth from the tomb: the chick bursting from its shell; the bursting pomegranate—a symbol of the power of our Lord, who was able to burst the tomb on Easter Day and come forth alive.

## Materials

Seeds, paper towels, and bottle; paper, styrofoam, pencil or dry pall-point pen, paint.

## Activities

1. *Planting seeds*

LOOK AT SOME DEAD LOOKING SEEDS — PLANT THEM and WATCH THE EASTER CHANGE! RESURRECTION

Roll a paper towel into a tube and insert it into a thin bottle such as those olives come in. Put ½" of water in the bottom of the jar. Stick some popping corn kernels between the glass and the towel. Watch for the RESURRECTION as the seeds sprout and come to life

## 2. Symbol making for Easter greetings

THINK of a NEW SYMBOL THAT SAYS resurrection THIS YEAR. USE IT TO MAKE SOME EASTER GREETING CARDS.

EASTER

Trace your symbol onto a piece of styrofoam. (You can buy it in sheets at a hardware store or lumber yard, or use a piece that came packed with an appliance.)

Use a pencil or dry ball point pen to indent the design into the foam. Spread paint on the entire surface of the foam, and press onto paper.

A POMEGRANATE

AN EGG

A BUTTERFLY

37

# 16. ASCENSION DAY

And it came to pass, while He blessed them, He was parted from them, and carried up into heaven. Luke 24:51 KJV

## A Talk with the Children

May 15 is an important festival day in Germany. Schools are closed, and shops and businesses too. In America it is often ignored by most people.

Before His ascension our Lord and Savior Jesus Christ instructed His disciples to take the Gospel to all people, to baptize them in the name of the Father, Son, and Holy Spirit. Jesus promised to send the Holy Spirit, and that He would be with His disciples always.

## Materials

Balloons, helium, plastic dry cleaner bag, soda straws, candles, cellophane tape.

## Activities

1. *Balloon ascension*

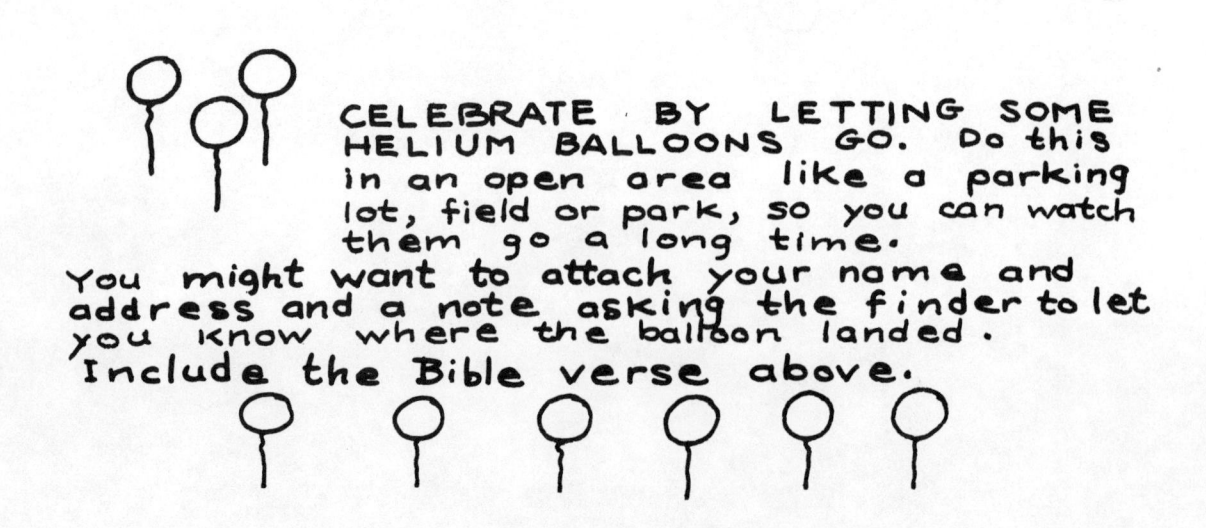

CELEBRATE BY LETTING SOME HELIUM BALLOONS GO. Do this in an open area like a parking lot, field or park, so you can watch them go a long time. You might want to attach your name and address and a note asking the finder to let you know where the balloon landed. Include the Bible verse above.

## 2. Bag kite

**TO BE DONE ONLY WITH ADULT SUPERVISION:**
(THIS MIGHT BE FUN FOR YOUR WHOLE CHURCH SCHOOL CLASS at a picnic supper.)

Materials: A thin plastic dry cleaner bag with no holes
Plastic soda straws
cellophane tape
a box of small birthday cake candles.

READ ACTS 1: 6 to 11

- tape 4 straws firmly into an X
- punch holes into the top side of the straws — big enough to hold the candles.
- tape the dry cleaner bag's open edge to the four ends of the straws.

TAPE THE TOP HOLE SHUT

- Poke the candles into the holes in the straws so they point toward the top of the plastic bag. BE SURE NONE IS SO CLOSE THE BAG CAN CATCH ON FIRE.

- One child can hold each corner of the X while AN ADULT LIGHTS the CANDLES. watch the bag inflate as the candles heat the air. When it is fully inflated let go and watch it ASCEND!

IMAGINE WHAT IT WAS LIKE TO WATCH CHRIST ASCEND!

39

# 17.
# PENTECOST
*The Birthday of the Christian Church*

And they were all filled with the Holy Spirit, and began to speak in other tongues, as the Spirit gave them utterance. Acts 2:4 RSV

## A Talk with the Children

Christians have had many kinds of places to worship in—homes, caves, tents, stores, catacombs, battlefields, cathedrals.

The first worship service (after Jesus' ascension) was held in the streets of Jerusalem by the disciples, and Peter preached a sermon.

We can read all aout it in the second chapter of the Book of Acts.

## Materials

Small boxes, cardboard, glue, scissors, paint.

## Activities

1. *Models of church buildings through the ages*
2. *Time line chart of drawings*

Gather up small boxes, cardboard, glue, scissors, paints, and other materials and make some models of some of these places.

OR: MAKE A TIME LINE CHART on a long piece of shelf paper. Begin with Pentecost and draw a series of pictures of church kinds of places, ending with your own church—this year.

YOU MIGHT OFFER TO DISPLAY YOUR CREATION AT CHURCH ON PENTECOST.

At home or in the library, see how many languages you can find the Bible written in. How would it sound to hear people reading all those languages at once.

You might have a Pentecost birthday party and invite each participant to read the Pentecost story in a different language.

"Und als der Tag der Pfingsten erfüllt war...."

"Og da Pintsesestens Dag var kommen..."

"Le jour de la Pentecôte étant arrivé...."

"Y cuando hubo venido cumplidamente el día de Pentecostés..."

Read Acts 2 — or at least the first 12 verses.

# 18.
# ARBOR DAY
*April 22—in many states*

And he shall be like a tree planted by the rivers of waters, that bringeth forth his fruit in his season; his leaf also shall not wither, and whatsoever he doeth shall prosper. Psalm 1:3 KJV

**A Talk with the Children**

Trees are beautiful. They use our carbon dioxide (that we exhale) and give us back oxygen that we need. We are partners with trees. Fruits and nuts grow on trees, which we enjoy eating.

Our activity should be to *plant a tree* somewhere. Perhaps we can find a place and get permission to plant one as a class in our schoolyard or churchyard.

We should each ask our parents if the family could plant one in our yard, especially one that blossoms in the spring, and may bear fruit in the winter.

Sometimes our state forestry department or city parks department will give us seedlings or small trees to plant.

♧♧♧♧♧♧♧♧♧

# MOTHER'S DAY (May)
# FATHER'S DAY (June)

Honor thy father and mother, which is the first commandment with promise, that it may be well with thee, and thou mayest live long on the earth. Ephesians 6:23 KJV

# ADOPT A TREE

KEEP A RECORD OF A TREE....
KEEP A SCRAP BOOK RECORD OF THE TREE'S CHANGES.

🍃 PLANT A TREE
- ON THE ANNIVERSARY OF YOUR BAPTISM
- ON YOUR CONFIRMATION DAY
- ON ARBOR DAY - APRIL 22.

*HI, TREE!*

🍃 ASK SOMEONE TO TAKE YOUR PICTURE IN FRONT OF THE TREE EVERY YEAR ON THAT SAME DAY. YOU'LL BOTH GROW AND THE RECORD WILL BE FUN TO WATCH.

🍃 MAKE A RUBBING OF THE BARK. PLACE A PIECE OF PAPER OVER THE BARK AND TAPE IN PLACE WITH MASKING PAPER STRIPS THAT GO ALL THE WAY AROUND THE TRUNK. HOLDING A THICK CRAYON ON ITS SIDE, RUB GENTLY OVER THE ENTIRE PAPER. MAKE SEVERAL RUBBINGS. MAKE SOME MORE IN A FEW YEARS AND COMPARE THEM. HOW HAS YOUR TREE CHANGED?

🍃 PHOTOGRAPH YOUR TREE EVERY MONTH OR SO. COMPARE THE PICTURES. LOOK FOR CHANGES. EXAMINE THE TIPS OF THE BRANCHES EACH TIME. WHAT DIFFERENCES DO YOU SEE?

🍃 HANG SOME LEAVES BY A THREAD IN YOUR WINDOW. PUT SOME IN YOUR RECORD.

When does your tree BLOOM? Keep a record of the date. Is it the same every year? What makes it change?

🍃 BUY A YARD OF TRANSPARENT PLASTIC SUCH AS CONTACT. COLLECT SEVERAL LEAVES FROM YOUR TREE IN SPRING, SEVERAL IN SUMMER, AND AGAIN IN FALL. EACH TIME PEEL AWAY SOME OF THE BACKING FROM THE PLASTIC AND CAREFULLY LAY THE LEAVES ON THE STICKY SIDE. PRESS ANOTHER PIECE OF FILM ON TOP (so the leaf is like the filling in a sandwich.) NOW CUT OUT THE LEAVES LEAVING 1/4" plastic all around the edges.

# ♥ MOTHER'S DAY ♥
# FATHER'S DAY

### A Talk with the Children

Let's talk about different ways we can honor and help our parents on their special days, and all through the year.

I don't have to tell you that they love you more than anyone else does, and that they care about you, and give you the things you need: like food and clothes, and take you to church and Sunday school.

They brought you to Jesus and made you a child of God at your baptism.

Here are some ideas for celebrating parents. You can think of others.

Celebrate with your parents and have a "This Is Your Life" party. Get little secrets about them from your grandparents and your uncles and aunts, and surprise them.

If your out-of-town friends or relatives can't come, write to them and ask them to write back about your parents and their life together.

Celebrate with a "Parent-of-the-Year" party. Make up a loving cup and award it with a speech. Make up coupons for jobs—IOU's—promising to do extra work around the house.

Make up a family photo album from snapshots before you were born, and include vacations, and first day at school, and party photographs.

What other good ideas do you have for showing your parents how much you love them?

# 19. TRINITY

*The First Sunday After Pentecost*

The grace of the Lord Jesus Christ, and the love of God, and the communion of the Holy Ghost be with you all. 2 Corinthians 13:14 KJV

## A Talk with the Children

There is a familiar legend about St. Patrick and the shamrock that has caused this leaf to be used as symbol for the Trinity. Triangles and interwoven circles are most often used. Patrick was a missionary among the pagans of Ireland. To prove that the Father, Son, and Holy Spirit are three Persons, yet one in essence, he used the lowly leaf of this plant to explain "one in three."

## Materials

Cardboard, string, construction paper, scissors, colored pencils or pens.

## Activity

*Making Trinity mobiles*

Use the triangle as basic design. Cut a triangle out of cardboard, each side 12 inches long. Punch a hole at each point.

Draw strings or ribbons or cord through each hole, tie together at top (about 12-inch lengths) and at lower end of each string attach a symbol that you choose for each of the Persons in the Trinity.

Instead of one triangle, you could use three. Or use three interlocking circles for your basic Trinity symbol.

TIE one symbol to the end of each string.

CHRIST:
the fish
the cross
the chi-rho

HOLY SPIRIT:
the dove
seven flames

FATHER:
an eye
a hand

THE CIRCLE MEANS ETERNITY BECAUSE IT HAS NO BEGINNING AND NO ENDING, LIKE GOD

# 20. FLAG DAY

*June 14*

Blessed is the nation whose God is the Lord, and the people whom He hath chosen for His own inheritance. Psalm 33:12 KJV

## A Talk with the Children

June 14 is the anniversary of the adoption of the American flag in 1777. On January 2, 1776, the first flag of the United States was raised at Cambridge, Massachusetts, by George Washington. Each of the thirteen colonies had had its own flag. The Grand Union flag consisted of 13 alternating red and white stripes with a blue canton bearing the crosses of St. George and St. Andrew.

The flag that was adopted by the Congress in 1977 changed it to 13 white stars in a blue field.

The story of Betsy Ross and the first flag is now somewhat discredited; there are no official records to confirm that she was responsible for the design and making of the first flag.

## Materials

Paper, scissors, crayons, colored pencils.

## Activities

Make some paper flags of all the stars and stripes flags since the first one with 13 stars.

Locate a U.S. flag with 48 stars (before Alaska and Hawaii became states).

What is the design and what are the symbols in *your state's flag?*

*Make a personal flag* for you or your family. Enlarge it. Use it as a pattern to cut parts out of different colored fabrics. Glue together, or sew together.

# 21. CLASS BANNER

No man, when he hath lighted a candle, putteth it in a secret place, neither under a bushel, but on a candlestick, that they which come in may see the light. Luke 11:33 KJV

### A Talk with the Children

Long ago, important families and clans were identified by symbols. These designs were embroidered on people's clothes and dyed or painted on banners and flags. They were used to show who was who in battles and sports competitions. Today many schools, churches, companies, and other institutions use these small designs, called logos, on rings, letter paper, books, products, and so on. In Japan they are still used on banners. They have been used there for centuries, and were probably also used in central Europe from about the 12th century.

Banners are used to publicly tell everyone who you are and what you think is important.

### Materials

Any material, paper or cloth.
Yarn, colored thread or string.

### Activities

Everyone in class could contribute a piece of fabic, bringing it from home. *A patchwork banner* could be made from all the pieces, sewing these together.

You could choose a class name or motto and stitch with yarn on felt or monk's cloth, or glue cut-out pieces of felt onto felt.

Try to keep designs simple.
Think of other reasons to make banners.

MAKE A PATCHWORK BANNER WITH ALL THESE PIECES. SEW ON A BACKING.

YOU COULD CHOOSE A CLASS NAME and/or LOGO to put on your banner.

Braid or SINGLE CROCHET A CHAIN from yarn in your class colors. DRAW THE DESIGN ON THE BANNER AND OUTLINE IT WITH GLUE — press on the YARN braid or crochet. (If you want to wash your banner, sew instead of glue.) KEEP YOUR DESIGN VERY SIMPLE.

THINK of some WAYS TO USE YOUR BANNER.
Could you:
- hang it outside your door?
- take it on field trips? Hang it to show where to meet.
- parades 
- school games
- picnics
- field meets

IF THAT WAS FUN, MAKE ANOTHER BANNER
- FOR YOUR FAMILY
- FOR YOURSELF — for your own door
- FOR A BROTHER or SISTER or COUSIN for CHRISTMAS —
- FOR A NEW BABY

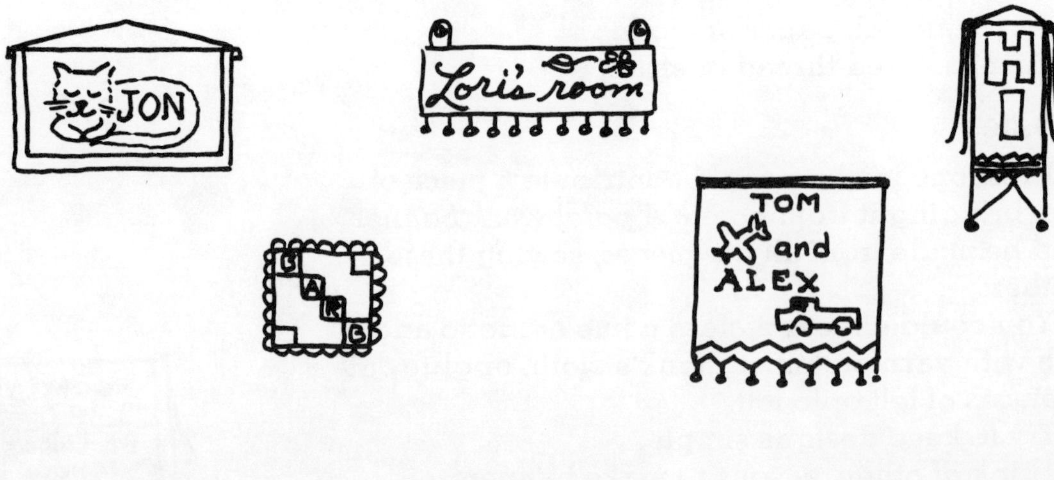

# 22. MAKE A MOBILE

The wind bloweth where it listeth, and thou hearest the sound thereof, but cannot tell whence it cometh and whither it goeth; so is everyone that is born of the Spirit. John 3:8 KJV

**A Talk with the Children**

Look up the definition of the word kinetics. It simply means: motion; of, relating to, or produced by motion. Perhaps you will find another word: kinescope—in your dictionary. It was first used with motion pictures. It is the technical word for the cathode-ray tube in your television set that changes the electrical signal into the pictures on your TV screen.

There are many forms of art in addition to painting, drawing, and sculpture. One form is called mobiles. In this century Naum Gabo and Marcel Duchamp were the first artists to make mobiles. The most popular artist who constructed mobiles was Alexander Calder. The most common form is an object that moves in air currents, by a breeze outdoors or in your room. Some mobiles move in water and by sound waves.

**Materials**

Almost any material can be used, including styrofoam trays, aluminum wrap, tin, wood, paper, cardboard; wire; and thread.

**Activities**

SAVE SOME STYROFOAM MEAT TRAYS, CUPS and DISHES.

CUT THEM INTO ☆ SIMPLE SHAPES WITH SCISSORS OR A STENCIL KNIFE.

⌂ ♡ ☆ 🎃 HOLIDAY SHAPES ◇ ♡ I ✚ ◉

ANN 21 — NUMBERS AND LETTERS

↪ PAINT THE SHAPES WITH ACRYLIC PAINTS
WAIT TILL ONE SIDE IS DRY — TURN OVER AND PAINT THE
OTHER SIDE — MAYBE THE NEXT DAY.
work on wax paper — try to make your paint neat.

↪ HANG THE SHAPES WITH A NEEDLE AND
THREAD or NYLON FISH LINE. ↪ from a cup
a strip
a circle

↪ HANG THE MOBILE
IN AN AIR CURRENT
MADE WHEN A DOOR
OPENS AND CLOSES or
THE FURNACE GOES ON.

↪ MAKE A SET of MATH FACT MOBILES
TO HANG ACROSS YOUR ROOM.
MEMORIZE THEM JUST BEFORE
YOU FALL TO SLEEP.

Pleasant dreams!

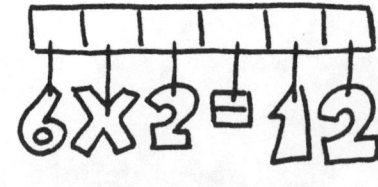

RIDDLE:
HOW IS A MOBILE LIKE PEOPLE WHO LOVE GOD?
Look for the answer in your Bible —
Psalm 103, verses 15 to 18

50

# 23. POUFF BALLS

And the Lord God formed man of the dust of the ground. Genesis 2:7 KJV

## A Talk with the Children

In some ways, people are much alike. In other ways we are all very different. It is fun to see what different ideas we can have starting from the same base. Let's learn to make pouff balls and then see how many different things we can think of to do with them.

## Materials

Tissue paper, glue, scissors.

## Activity

1. Cut out ten tissue paper circles, same size, about three inches in diameter. Use at least two colors. A bracelet or a round piece of cardboard makes a good stencil.
2. Fold each circle in half and then open again.
3. Put the circles in a pile alternating colors. Use at least two colors.
4. Use needle and thread to sew ten circles together along the centerfold. Or use a staple.
5. Fold the whole pile into a half circle.
6. Open the top half circle like a book. Drop a spot of white glue (with a toothpick) on the edge of the circle (at about three o'clock).
7. Fold the next half circle down onto the spot of glue. Press together. Put a drop of glue at the two and four positions of numbers on a clock.
8. Fold the next half circle onto these two dots of glue. Press together. Put one dot of glue at three o'clock onto this half circle.
9. Continue folding down the half circles and placing dots of glue, alternating the 3 o'clock position with the 2/4 position.

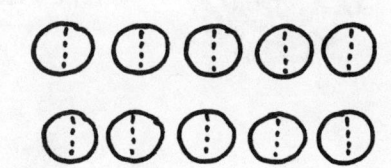

⑩ WAIT! LET THE GLUE DRY THOROUGHLY.

⑪ OPEN GENTLY. YOU MAY NEED TO CAREFULLY PRY OPEN SOME OF THE HOLES WITH A PENCIL. THE OPEN POUFF BALL WILL FORM A HALF SPHERE. IF YOU WANT A WHOLE BALL, PASTE TWO TOGETHER BACK TO BACK.

Try sandwiching a larger circle cut into flower petals in between. What can you find for a stem?
- coat hanger wire
- dowel
- soda straw

You could set your flower into a pretty paper cup of sand or plaster — what a nice favor or decoration!

⑫ If you aren't making a flower, GLUE YOUR POUFF BALL TO A CIRCLE OF CONSTRUCTION PAPER OR ANYTHING ELSE YOU'D LIKE TO DECORATE. GLUE ONE HALF AT A TIME

CUT EYES, EARS, MOUTHS, TAILS, etc. FROM HEAVIER PAPER, AND GLUE THEM ON. BE GENTLE AND PATIENT!

You can hang pouff balls with a thread fastened with a drop of glue — or poked through the ball by a needle.

You can glue a pouff ball on the fold of a card. It will hide till the card is opened!

shut — Happy Birthday to Mom
open — I Love you from Mary

WHO WOULD LIKE TO HAVE ONE OF YOUR POUFF BALL CREATIONS FOR A GIFT?

COULD YOUR CLASS OR CLUB MAKE SOME FOR A NURSING HOME OR TO TAKE TO SHUT-INS FROM YOUR CHURCH?

shut — Seek and you shall find knock and it will be opened to you!
open — JOY TO YOU TODAY!

MATTHEW 7:7

# 24. FRIENDSHIP ALBUM

Peace be to thee. Our friends salute thee. Greet the friends by name. 3 John 15 KJV

### A Talk with the Children

When you grow older, you will want to remember your friends.

You will want to think of the good times you had with your friends at school and your friends in your neighborhood.

You can collect photos of them in an album.

You can also collect their thoughts and information about them by writing or having them write facts about themselves.

### Materials

Blank notebooks, photo album.
Papers stapled or sewn together.

### Activity

Trade your school pictures with your friends.

Mount them with plastic stick-down corners on a page in a blank album.

Have each friend write something in your book, signing his/her name.

Add things you would like to remember about them, or have them write what they would like you to remember about them.

# COLLECT A FRIENDSHIP ALBUM

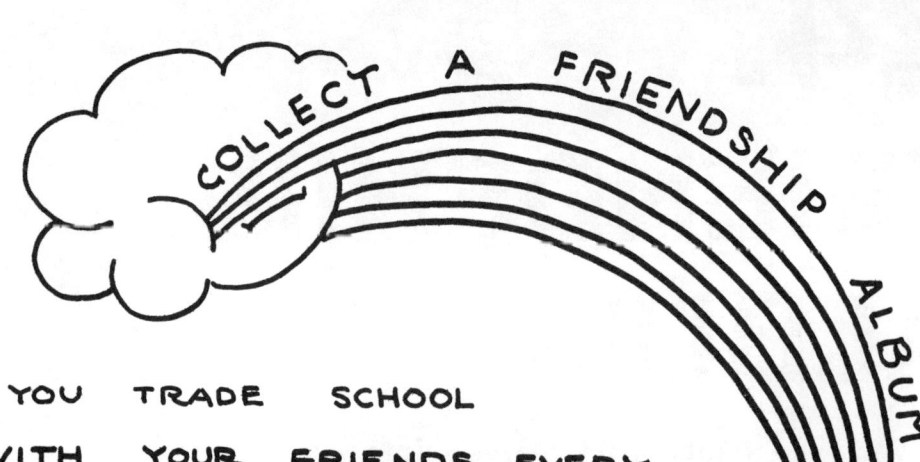

IF YOU TRADE SCHOOL PICTURES WITH YOUR FRIENDS EVERY YEAR, PUT THEM INTO A NOTEBOOK WITH LITTLE STICK-DOWN CORNERS, OR INTO PLASTIC PHOTO PAGES IN A BINDER OF SOME SORT. ADD THINGS YOU WOULD LIKE TO REMEMBER ABOUT YOUR FRIENDS:

- AGE
- BIRTH DATE
- ADDRESS
- PHONE
- GRADE
- FAVORITE COLOR
- FAVORITE FOOD
- FAVORITE GAMES
- HOBBY

WHAT ELSE WOULD YOU LIKE TO REMEMBER?

HAVE YOUR FRIENDS WRITE A PARAGRAPH IN YOUR BOOK, AND THEN SIGN THEIR NAMES.

HOW MUCH FUN IT WILL BE TO LOOK BACK AT THIS BOOK WHEN YOU ARE OLDER TO SEE HOW EVERYONE HAS CHANGED!

# 25. ONCE UPON A TIME

*Telling a Bible Story*

And great multitudes were gathered together unto Him, so that He went into a ship, and sat; and the whole multitude stood on the shore. And He spake many things unto them in parables. Matthew 13.2-3 KJV

## A Talk with the Children

People like to tell stories, and everybody likes to hear stories. Today most of us read stories in books and magazines; but more of us enjoy stories on television.

Five hundred years ago few people read. Then Johann Gutenberg (a German printer) invented a process for setting type by hand and printing paper with ink. There is evidence that printing was done in China and Korea before that time.

People learned from others through storytelling. Even today there are primitive peoples who have no written language. They learn through spoken words and picture language. How many ways are there to tell a story?

## Materials

Paper, pencils, crayon or paint, boxes, dowels, cardboard, table.

## Activities

1. Just *tell the story as people used to do.* Let your listeners use their imaginations to "see" the characters. Be very dramatic, change your voice to suit the character.

2. *Puppet theater.* Make stick puppets—draw characters on paper and cut out; or cut pictures

—behind the card table

from a clothing catalog or magazines. Paste on cardboard—tape onto a popsicle stick. Turn a cardtable on its side or sit on the floor behind a desk or chest. Hold the puppets along the top edge, moving them as you tell the story. Change your voice, or have different people speak the parts.

3. *Television.* Draw pictures of the story in sequence like a comic strip. Paste them on a long strip of paper such as shelf paper. Cut a hole in one side of a grocery carton. Cut two small holes at the top corners, insert dowels through each hole. Wind the strip of paper with pictures (have an unused section at each end) around one of the dowels, fasten with tape or thumbtacks.

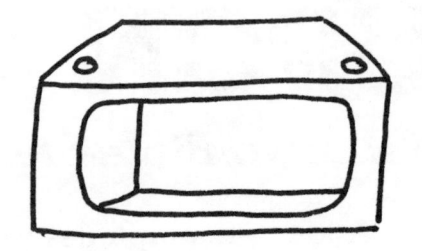

Fasten the other end to the other dowel. As you turn the dowels, stop each picture at the cutout "screen," and tell a part of the story. You can record your voice, and add music, too.

4. *Draw a picture book.* Staple the pages together. Let the pictures tell the story. Do not print any words in your picture book, and do not *tell* the story.

5. *Movie.* Perhaps your school, or someone's parents, have a movie camera. Write a script, make costumes, direct actors, and film your story as a moving picture. Silent movies: print explanations and dialog. You can record voices on tape and play it synchronized with the movie.

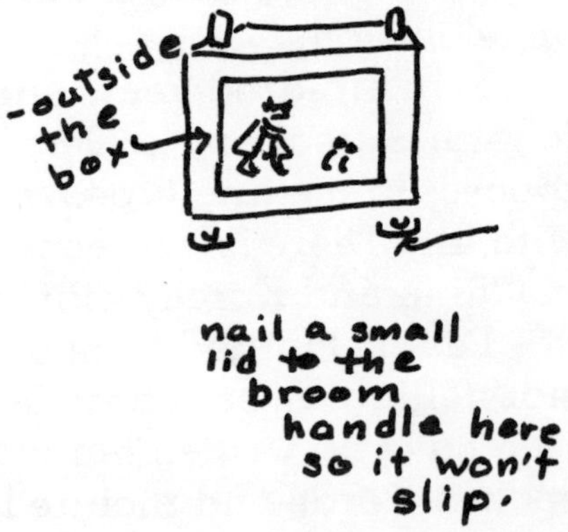

6. *Slides.* Write a script, make costumes, photograph in color, and project (with or without recorded voices).

7. Have prints enlarged from your photographs, mount them in a display or paste them in sequence in book form.

How many ways can you *tell* a Bible story?

Could you do a book report for your class at school this way? — tell a Bible story to your Sunday School class?

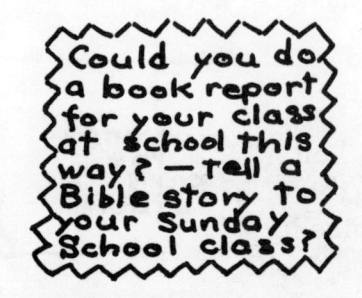

56

# 26.
# LET'S PRETEND

When I was a child, I spake as a child, I understood as a child, I thought as a child: but when I became a man, I put away childish things.
1 Corinthians 13:11 KJV

### A Talk with the Children

Do you know someone you wish to be like? What would you like to be when you grow up? Some things people do require a great deal of study and practice. For instance, doctors and teachers go to school for 16 or 20 years. They continue learning new things all the time they are working.

"Let's Pretend" is a game that requires imagination. If you admire someone, or you want to be like them, you can pretend to be them for a few minutes. Try it.

### Materials

Paper, pencil, old clothes, costumes, biographies.

### Activities

1. Is there someone you would like to be when you grow up? Is there a job or profession that interests you? Do you want to be a nurse or secretary? an astronaut? a scientist? a lawyer? a firefighter? a crime fighter? a computer programmer? a pastor? a ballet dancer? a musician? Investigate in books and college catalogs or stories in magazines and newspapers and make a list of what subjects you will need to take in schools, how many hours you will have to practice, what disciplines you will have to learn.

*Write a report* on "What I Have to Do to Become _____."

Why do you think this work is important?
How does it help people?

2. Is there someone you admire? *Write a composition* about them. Your mother or father? brother or sister? teacher or pastor? uncle or aunt? *Talk* about them: what they do, why you admire them.

3. *Pretend you are—*
. your dad
   when you have lost or misplaced one of his tools
   when you have helped him with a project;
. your mom
   when you bring home an especially good school paper
   when you drag in a lot of mud on your shoes;
. your sister or brother
   when you loan him/her something you value
   when you break something of hers/his;
. your teacher
   when the class is noisy, inattentive, and disrespectful
   when a lot of the kids have brought a bouquet of dandelions on the same day.

**At Home**

For Hallowe'en — or just for fun — find things around the House to make up your own costume.
WHAT ELSE CAN YOU PRETEND TO BE?

IF YOUR FRIENDS MAKE COSTUMES TOO, HAVE A PARADE AROUND THE BLOCK WITH WAGONS, BIKES and PETS!

# 27.
# AFTER SCHOOL HOURS

And that from a child thou has known the Holy Scriptures, which are able to make thee wise unto salvation through faith which is in Christ Jesus. 2 Timothy 3:15 KJV

## A Talk with the Children

What do you like to do after school? What do your friends do? Ask your parents and grandparents what they did.

What do you choose to do when the tasks adults choose for you are done—your schoolwork and housework tasks? Look at the way you spend your free time and decide if it is helping you grow into the kind of person you choose to be. Are there some things you would like to try that you have never done before?

Try three new things this month.

## Materials

Pencil and paper.

## Activities

Some suggestions:

*Join* a scout troop: Bluebirds, Cub Scouts, Brownies.

*Join* in on an athletic program at the local Y—swimming, basketball, etc.

*Take lessons:* Learning to play a musical instrument, dance class, art class, etc.

*Start a hobby:* Photography, stamp collecting, model building (planes or cars), pottery, embroidery, knitting, doll house furniture, junk sculpture (wood, cloth, tin, iron, metals, etc.).

Learn to *help mom with cooking or baking.*

*Amy and April's Grandma liked to make rooms of a house on wrapping paper. She showed them how to paste magazine pictures of furniture on a house shape.*

And ... learn to do things for others without expecting something from them in return—not just helping your parents cleaning up and picking up, but *cutting grass, raking leaves, gardening, car washing, etc.*

And ... *getting to know all the people on your block.*

Are there *older people?* Sometimes they live alone. Visit them, introduce yourself, drop greeting cards at their doors. Bring them gifts, especially something you have made yourself. All the things that you help with around the house have to be done in their homes too. Offer to do it. Let their thanks be payment enough.

NOW ... *Make a list of things to do after school hours—*
. for myself
. for my parents (and brothers and sisters)
. with my friends
. for my neighbors.

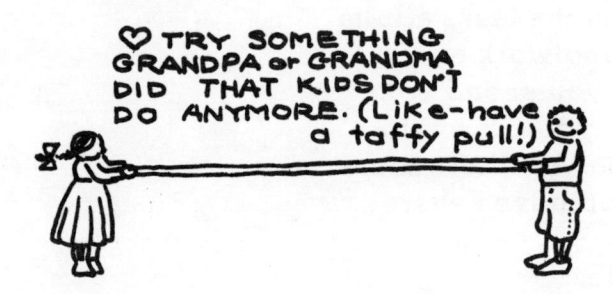

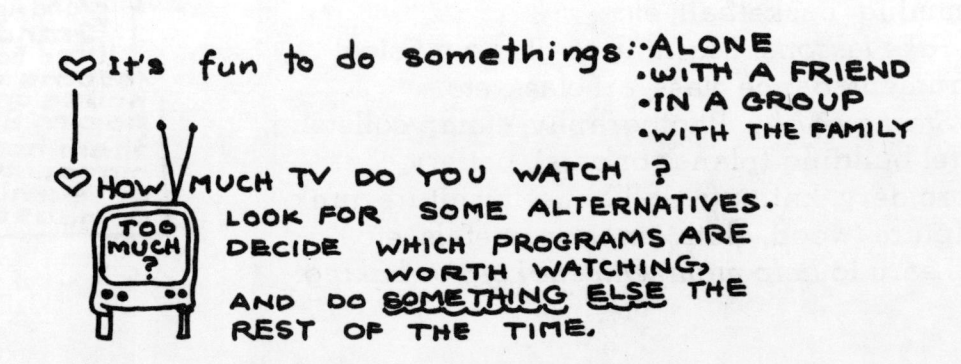

TRY 3 NEW THINGS THIS MONTH.
1........
2........
3........

♡ TRY SOMETHING GRANDPA or GRANDMA DID THAT KIDS DON'T DO ANYMORE. (Like - have a taffy pull!)

♡ It's fun to do somethings: • ALONE
• WITH A FRIEND
• IN A GROUP
• WITH THE FAMILY

♡ HOW MUCH TV DO YOU WATCH? LOOK FOR SOME ALTERNATIVES. DECIDE WHICH PROGRAMS ARE WORTH WATCHING, AND DO SOMETHING ELSE THE REST OF THE TIME.

# 28. BOOK CARE

*(Paper covers)*

Give instruction to a wise man, and he will be yet wiser; teach a just man, and he will increase in learning. Proverbs 9:9 KJV

## A Talk with the Children

Do you have some books that you take home from school every day?

Take good care of your books. They are gifts from the past.

They will help you learn and will help you be what you want to be.

They come from God's creation, from the earth, from trees and other resources, minerals, and energy.

We can help protect them from wear and tear.

## Materials

Heavy paper (brown wrapping paper is best); scissors; colors: pencils, paints, crayons; transparent tape; clear contact plastic.

## Activity

This is a fun-to-do project for classroom or home that will help to protect books from being damaged from much usage.

Lay your book open on a heavy piece of paper (a grocery bag will do) that has been cut six inches wider and four inches longer than your book.

Draw lines from the edge of the book's spine to the edge of the paper.

Remove the book and decorate the paper cover with designs and colors, incorporating these with the title or the subject. Use pencils, markers, paints, etc.

Cover the whole paper cover with transparent plastic such as contact.

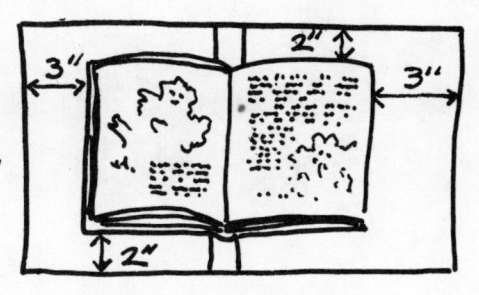

Cut along the four lines drawn and fold the two flaps into the center on the under side of the paper. You may need to trim more away.

Replace the book. Open it to the front cover, and fold in the paper edges. Tape them carefully in place. Do the same to the back cover.

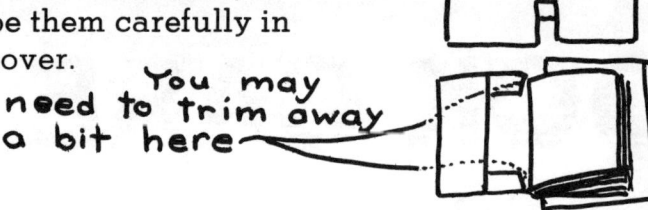

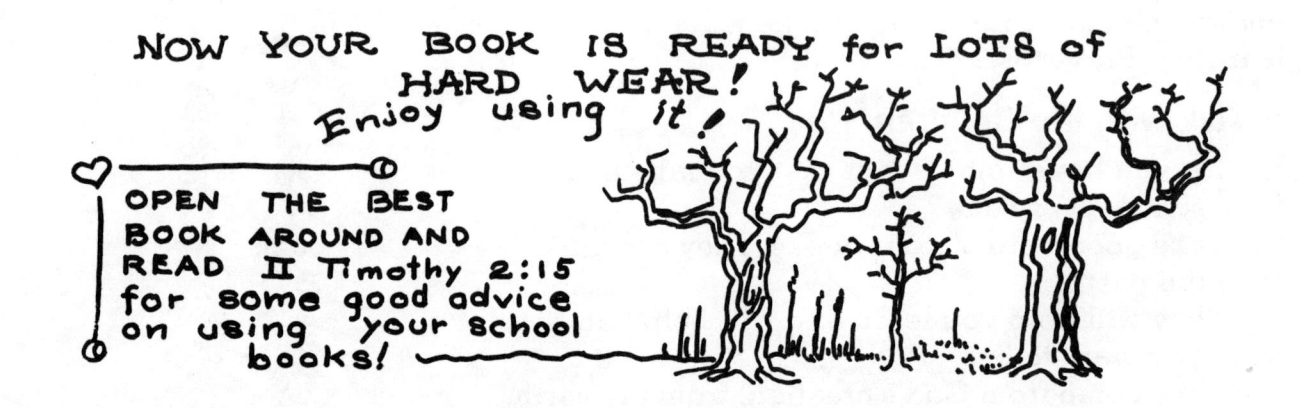

You may need to trim away a bit here

NOW YOUR BOOK IS READY for LOTS of HARD WEAR! Enjoy using it!

OPEN THE BEST BOOK AROUND AND READ II Timothy 2:15 for some good advice on using your school books!

# 29. SCHOOL DAYS

Let no man despise thy youth, but be thou an example of the believers, in word, in conversation, in charity, in spirit, in faith, in purity. 1 Timothy 4:12 KJV

## A Talk with the Children

It's fun to keep records of things we do and say, how we look and how we feel about what happens to us. It's even more fun to look at those records a few, or many, years later and see how we have changed. Frequently we find many things recorded we would have otherwise forgotten. A box for school papers, programs, and other souvenirs, a diary or journal, a photo album, are all ways of keeping memories safe. The end of each school year is a good time to make such a record.

## Materials

Paper and pencil or pen.

## Activity

*Putting down some facts about myself, today!*

WHAT DO YOU LIKE BEST ABOUT SCHOOL?
WHAT DO YOU LIKE LEAST ABOUT SCHOOL?

MY FAVORITE TEACHER HAS BEEN: _ _ _ _ _ _ _ _ _ _ _ _
MY FAVORITE SUBJECT HAS BEEN: _ _ _ _ _ _ _ _ _ _ _ _
A GOOD TIME I REMEMBER IS: _ _ _ _ _ _ _ _ _ _ _ _
_ _ _ _ _ _ _ _ _ _ _ _ _ _ _ _ _ _ _ _ _ _ _ _ _ _ _
A HARD TIME I REMEMBER IS: _ _ _ _ _ _ _ _ _ _ _ _
_ _ _ _ _ _ _ _ _ _ _ _ _ _ _ _ _ _ _ _ _ _ _ _ _ _ _
MY BEST FRIENDS IN FIRST GRADE WERE: _ _ _ _ _
_ _ _ _ _ _ _ _ _ _ _ _ _ _ _ _ _ _ _ _ _ _ _ _ _ _ _
SECOND GRADE:
THIRD GRADE:
FOURTH GRADE:
FIFTH GRADE:
SIXTH GRADE:
MY FAVORITE SCHOOL MENU: _ _ _ _ _ _ _ _ _ _ _
_ _ _ _ _ _ _ _ _ _ _ _ _ _ _ _ _ _ _ _ _ _ _ _ _ _ _
SOMETHING NEW I LEARNED THIS WEEK: _ _ _ _ _ _
_ _ _ _ _ _ _ _ _ _ _ _ _ _ _ _ _ _ _ _ _ _ _ _ _ _ _
A SONG I LEARNED: _ _ _ _ _ _ _ _ _ _ _ _ _ _ _
AN ART PROJECT I ENJOYED: _ _ _ _ _ _ _ _ _ _ _
MY FAVORITE LIBRARY BOOK: _ _ _ _ _ _ _ _ _ _ _
MY FAVORITE SPORT: _ _ _ _ _ _ _ _ _ _ _ _ _ _ _
MY MOST ENJOYABLE AFTER SCHOOL PASTIME: _ _ _ _ _
_ _ _ _ _ _ _ _ _ _ _ _ _ _ _ _ _ _ _ _ _ _ _ _ _ _ _
SOMETHING I DON'T LIKE TO DO, BUT DO ANYWAY—
    (cheerfully, we hope!) _ _ _ _ _ _ _ _ _ _ _ _

*Hurry, class, you're so slow!*

# 30. THE LAST WEEK OF SCHOOL

Train up a child in the way he should go, and when he is old, he will not depart from it. Proverbs 22:6 KJV

## A Talk with the Children

The last days of school can be a time for celebration.

Why not make it appreciation week? Let all the people who help to make your education possible know that you appreciate what they are doing for you? Your good school didn't just hapen. A lot of people had to go to school, and others have to work hard, to make it what it is.

Thank them!

## Materials

Drawing paper, colored pencils, paints, scissor, paste.

## Activity

*Make flower basket or greeting cards* for everybody to say THANKS.

# THE LAST DAY OF SCHOOL

WHY NOT TURN IT INTO AN APPRECIATION DAY FOR ALL THE PEOPLE WHO HELP MAKE YOUR GOOD EDUCATION POSSIBLE?

- cut a piece of drawing paper 6"x 8" mark off the end two inches for pasting. Lightly mark the center of the paper lengthwise, with pencil
- use many colors to draw a variety of flowers in the top half. Color the bottom half to look like a basket.
- cut out the flowers, and cut away the top half of the paste section. Be sure to leave the flowers attached to the basket.
- spread paste on the end section and curve the strip into a circle or basket shape. Hold the paste till it's dry enough to stick.
- Add a handle — ½" x 12" with paste or staples.
   - who will you make baskets for?
   - the cooks
   - the custodian
   - volunteers
   - office helpers — clerks
       — secretary
   - the principal
   - the nurse
   - special teachers
   - AND MOST importantly — your VERY OWN TEACHER.

66

# 31. AFTER SCHOOL IS OVER

And we know that all things work together for good to them that love God, to them who are called according to His purpose. Romans 8:28 KJV

## A Talk with the Children

How do you feel? now that school is almost over for this year?

Are you happy? sad? relieved? disappointed?

What kinds of things did you enjoy the most this school year? Which will you want to repeat next term? Which can you go on with at home during the summer vacation? Have you saved some keepsakes from school events?

## Materials

Pencil or pen, paper or notebook, box or folder; papers, programs, and souvenirs.

## Activity

*"This Is the Year That Was"*

A blank book that can be written and filled in with photographs, test papers, compositions, invitation, programs, etc., would be most practical. A sketch pad, notebook, or construction paper can be substituted, or a box if things are too bulky.

## How Do You Feel?

*What shall I put in my book?*

♡ Paste in YOUR BEST SCHOOL PAPERS

♡ Paste in pictures of FRIENDS and EVENTS you've ENJOYED.

♡ WRITE ABOUT YOUR FEELINGS: "I like my friend Tammy cause she always listens when I talk." "It felt good to get all my spelling words right."

♡ DRAW PICTURES OF THINGS YOU LIKE OR WANT TO REMEMBER. WRITE A STORY ABOUT THE PICTURE.

♡ WRITE DOWN SOME of your PRAYERS.

♡ WRITE ABOUT YOUR DREAMS.

♡ WRITE ABOUT YOUR FEELINGS. WHAT KINDS OF THINGS MAKE YOU:
- AFRAID ?
- HAPPY ?
- ANGRY ?
- SILLY ? etc.

# 32.
# SUMMER SOLSTICE

As snow in summer, and as rain in harvest, so honor is not seemly for a fool. Proverbs 26:1 KJV

## A Talk with the Children

Begin summer with a celebration.

When does summer begin for you? the day school is out? Memorial Day? July the Fourth? the day you go to camp? or to your grandparents for a vacation?

The summer solstice, when the sun is at its highest point over the Tropic of Cancer, occurs about June 22. This is the longest day of the year.

Scandinavian people sometimes celebrate midsummer day and might. At this time the sun remains visible for 24 hours (at the summer solstice) in the polar regions, along the Arctic Circle, 23½ degrees of latitude from the North Pole. This is called the midnight sun.

## Materials

Anything necessary for a parade or a picnic.

## Activity

Celebrate the summer solstice with a parade, a picnic, contests, a watermelon festival, ice cream social, costumes, a band.

# BEGIN SUMMER WITH A CELEBRATION!

GET YOUR FAMILY or FRIENDS TOGETHER TO CELEBRATE.

- Have a parade — decorate wagons, bikes, tricycles, baby strollers, PETS.
- wear costumes.
- play kazoos — choose a couple songs everybody knows, to march to.

END THE PARADE IN SOMEBODY'S BACK YARD WITH WATERMELON or ICE CREAM CONES.

Ask a neighbor who has no kids to judge costumes, and wheel-toy decorations for prizes.
Give out paper ribbons.

FASTEN with LOOPS OF MASKING TAPE.

Be sure **all** the little kids get prizes too.

## HAVE A PET SHOW.

CRAWLING PETS

Can your PET DO A TRICK FOR THE AUDIENCE?

Everyone can sit on lawn chairs while the pets are paraded before them.

# 33.
# VACATION

He shall have dominion also from sea to sea, and from the river unto the ends of the earth. Psalm 72:8 KJV

## A Talk with the Children

Where would you like to go for a summer vacation?

Does your family enjoy camping? visiting friends or relatives? traveling? going to the mountains? the seashore? to the zoo, parks, museums, the beach, the pool, Disneyland, Six Flags? or staying home?

## Materials

Pencil and paper; song.

## Activity

*Writing a third verse to the vacation song.*

# WHERE WOULD YOU LIKE TO GO FOR A SUMMER VACATION?

WRITE A THIRD VERSE TO THIS SONG ABOUT WHAT YOU WOULD LIKE TO SEE AND DO, WHERE YOU WOULD LIKE TO GO.

I like to go to the ci-ty To see the tall build-ings there. The el-e-va-tors go up so high I can't e-ven climb the stair!

I like to go to the country
To see the animals there,
The food that's growing green in the fields,
And maybe the County Fair!

# 34.
# BIRDS AND BUTTERFLIES

Behold the birds of the air, for they sow not, neither do they reap, nor gather into barns; yet your heavenly Father feedeth them. Matthew 6:26 KJV

## A Talk with the Children

In the summer when we are playing in the garden, parks, and playgrounds, we may be much more aware of nature. Of course, butterflies have grown out of their cocoons, and are dancing in the air. Baby birds are learning to fly.

We can be reminded of their beauty and the pleasure they bring all year round, when we see imitations of them in pictures, in glass, and in paintings.

We can make our own imitations.

## Materials

Colored tissue papers, hairpin or clothespin, white glue, feathers, paper, paints or inks, thread, liquid starch, fabric scraps.

## Activities

This can be a group or individual activity.

1. *Butterfly or bird made with tissue paper and pins.* Push a small piece of colored tissue paper, about 6" x 8", into a clothespin or bobbypin. A dot of glue on the inside of the pin will keep the paper from popping out. Hold till dry.

2. *Finger-paint* on one-half of a piece of folded paper, fold over, and press all over quickly while paint is still wet.

3. Use a medicine dropper to drop colors (ink or paint) on half of a folded piece of paper. Fold over and press. Allow to dry.

4. With the paper folded, *draw half a butterfly,* as large as the piece of paper will allow—the body is on the fold. Cut out the shape while it is still folded. Open and attach thread and hang.

5. *Cut birds and butterflies from thin fabric scraps.* Paint them with liquid starch. Iron dry. Hang with thread. Use needle, pin, or toothpick at center. You can stick another color fabric onto the wet starch and iron dry.

Your birds and butterflies can fly in the breezes on your porch, patio, or open window.

6. *Use a scrap of aluminum foil for the body* and attach with transparent tape various colored feathers. Hang from thread.

7. *Observe real butterflies.* Make a note of their size, designs, and colors of their wings. Look in a reference book to find their names. Moths and butterflies are different. Moths open their wings flat when resting. Butterflies have thin antennae.

You may want to *start a butterfly collection.* You will need a net, a killing jar, and pins and styrofoam for mounting in a framed box.

8. *Observe birds.* Describe them: color, size, shape. Check in a reference book for their names.

If you want to make a serious collection, get a
- net for catching, a
- killing jar,
- pins and styrofoam for mounting, and a
- framing box

AT A HOBBY STORE.

OTHERWISE JUST OBSERVE AND LET THESE BEAUTIFUL CREATURES HAVE THEIR FREEDOM UNHARMED.

CAN YOU MAKE UP A TUNE FOR THIS VERSE?

GOD MADE THE BUTTERFLIES TO FLY
ALTHOUGH THEY HAVE SIX LEGS.
THEY CRAWLED WHEN THEY WERE CATERPILLARS,
SAT, WHEN THEY WERE EGGS.

# 35. WATER PAINTINGS

And let him that is athirst, come; and whosoever will, let him take the water of life freely.
Revelation 22:17 KJV

## A Talk with the Children

God created many colors, add many shades of these colors. We can use our eyes to discover and enjoy colors. We can use paint to enjoy reproducing colors in many shapes and forms. Look about you and see how many you can find.

## Materials

Water, paints, brushes, clipboard, folding stool.

## Activities

1. *Water colors*

Water colors are extra fun because you can pack up a few things and walk out-of-doors on a nice day and find something to paint. Put some water in a jelly jar with a tight lid. Put a box of paints, a clipboard, paper, brushes in a sack or paper bag. Walk around until you find something you would like to paint a picture of. You might take along a folding stool. Water colors are especially good to do flowers, trees, and sky.

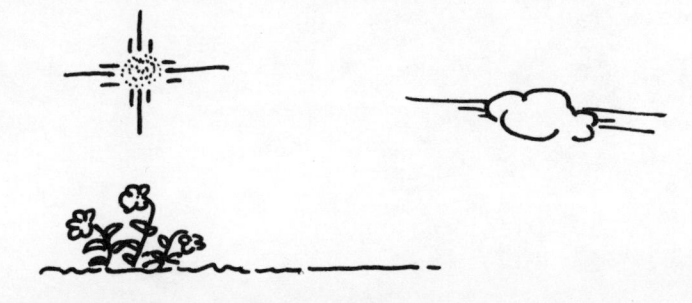

2. *Clear-water paintings*

Paint with clear water on the sidewalk, driveway, or patio. You'll need a bucket and a wide brush. You can watch your picture disappear. disappear.

### 3. *Chalk drawings*

Draw with chalk (the ordinary chalk used in school), the wider the better. Use concrete walks and walls, steps and streets. If you don't want to wait for the rain to wash it off, use the garden hose. Put on your swimming suit and double your water fun.

# 36. WINTER FLOWERS

Consider the lilies how they grow: they toil not ... and yet I say unto you that Solomon in all his glory was not arrayed like one of these. Luke 12:27 KJV

## A Talk with the Children

We can keep a small reminder of the summer—the places we visited, the good times we had there, and its trees and flowers. It's easy and it's fun to make things with dry flowers and colorful leaves.

## Materials

Flowers, leaves, ferns, cardboard, cloth, paper, plastic film, glue, toothpicks, picture frames with glass.

## Activities

Place flat flowers, ferns, and leaves between sheets of smooth paper towels and lay them between the pages of a big thick catalog or phone book. Put heavy books, or bricks, on top of the closed book. Wait a couple of weeks for the flowers to dry. Flowers that are too thick to lie flat can be taken apart, and each petal used.

Place your favorite *colored leaves* between two layers of plastic film (such a contact). Cut around them leaving 1/8" edge. Seal. Insert a needle and thread for *hanging* in a window, or anywhere.

Arrange some pressed flowers on a piece of cloth, paper, or thin cardboard. Attach leaves with white glue, applying with a toothpick. Cover both sides with clear plastic film. Punch hole at one end and insert loop of yarn for a tassle. Makes a great *bookmark* for you, or for gifts.

Can also use on lacy paper *doilies* or for table *place mats*.

Purchase some *small picture* frames with glass. Choose some dark-colored felt for a background; cut to size of frame. Make an arrangement with your flowers and ferns. Wash the glass and avoid putting your fingers on the under surface. Place it over your arrangement, add the frame. Turn over, add the cardboard backing, and tape. These will make beautiful additions to any room in your home, as well as attractive gifts.

Make a loose-leaf notebook into a *flower catalog*. Make an arrangement on the cover and cover that with plastic film. Place a flower or leaf on each page and identify each. Glue onto page, or cover with film.

IT'S FUN TO KEEP FLOWERS, FERNS, OR LEAVES FROM A FAVORITE PLACE OF TRIP FOR RECALLING WHEN WINTER COMES.

# NOTES

# NOTES